The Little Book of GOLF TRIVIA

by
Matt Lindsey
&
Raleigh Squires

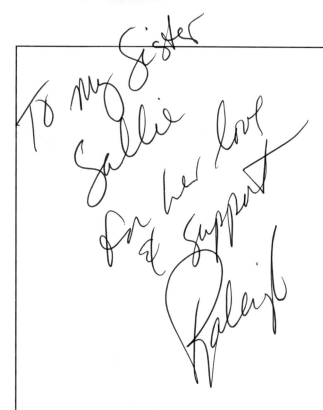

To my Sister Sallie for her love & support

Raleigh

© Copyright 1996. All rights reserved.

ACKNOWLEDGEMENTS

The information contained in this book was gathered from a variety of sources. We wish to thank ESPN, SportSouth, CBS, ABC, NBC, USA, and TBS television networks, ESPNNET, *USA Today*, *Golf Magazine*, and *Golf Digest* for their diligent coverage of the sport of golf. Thanks also go to the PGA, the USGA, and to Junior Golf and all the golf courses, pro shops, and driving ranges throughout the world for their promotion of the game itself. We would also like to especially thank Richard Courtney and the staff of EGGMAN Publishing for helping us do this.

INTRODUCTION

As avid golfers and fanatical fans of the sport, this compilation came about from love of the game. Many 19th hole conversations, after the birdies, bogeys, and bets are added up, center on information like what is contained herein. Now the conversation and competition can go on and on . . . and on.

With *The Little Book of Golf Trivia* we have tried to provide fun and entertainment for all golf enthusiasts, young and old, and to pay homage to those who have made the sport what it is today.

Origins of the Game

1. Where did the game of golf originate?

2. What were the first golf balls made of?

3. Who invented the first rubber-cored golf ball and when?

4. What is the oldest organized golf club?

5. When and where was the Royal and Ancient Club of St. Andrews founded?

Origins of the Game

6. When and where was golf introduced to the United States?

7. When and where was the first organized golf club in North America formed?

8. Who played the first documented round of golf in the U.S.?

9. What was the first golf club founded in the United States?

10. When and where did formal competition begin?

Origins of the Game

11. What is the governing body for golf in America?

12. In what year was the first golf course opened in the Soviet Union?

Origins of the Game

Answers

1. Some historians believe golf originated in Holland in the 1300s, although the Chinese Nationalist Golf Association claims it was played in China in the 3rd century B.C. Over the next 5 centuries on several continents, it evolved into the popular Scottish game then known as golfe, the direct ancestor of the modern game.
2. Feathers bound with leather
3. An American named Coburn Haskell, in 1899
4. The Honourable Company of Edinburgh Golfers is the first documented organized golf club although the Royal Burgess Golfing Society of Edinburgh claims to have been started 9 years earlier.
5. 1754, Fife, Scotland
6. In the mid-18th century in Charleston, South Carolina, and Virginia
7. The Royal Montreal Golf Club in Canada, 1873
8. In 1888, John Reid and friends laid out and played 6 holes on the Reid lawn in Yonkers, N.Y.
9. Both The Foxberg Golf Club, Clarion County, Pennsylvania, in 1887 and St. Andrews Golf Club of Yonkers, New York, in 1888 claim to be.
10. The first British Open in 1860 at Prestwick, Strathclyde in Scotland
11. The U.S.G.A. (United States Golf Association), founded in 1894
12. 1989

The British Open

1. Who won the first British Open?

2. Who has won the most British Open titles?

3. Who won the most consecutive British Opens?

4. What American golfer has won the most British Opens?

5. Who shot the lowest 9-hole score posted in the British Open?

The British Open

6. What is the lowest 18-hole score for any British Open?

7. Who holds the record for both the lowest 36-hole total and the lowest 54-hole total in the British Open?

8. What is the lowest 72-hole total score?

9. What three players in addition to Tom Morris, Jr. have won three successive British Open championships

10. Five other players have won back-to-back British Opens. Who are they?

The British Open

11. What two British Open champions have had sons who also won the British Opens?

12. Who were the youngest and oldest British Open champions?

13. Who was the only amateur to win the British Open?

14. Who won the 1995 British Open?

15. What is the playoff format for the British Open?

The British Open

Answers

1. Willie Park, Sr., 1860
2. Harry Vardon, 6, in 1896, 1898-99, 1908, 1911, and 1914
3. Tom Morris, Jr. 4, from 1868 to 1872 (It was not played in 1871.)
4. Tom Watson, 5, 1975, '77, '80, '82, and '83
5. 28 by Denis Durnian, first nine, second round, 1983, at Royal Birkdale
6. 63 by Mark Hayes, Turnberry, 1977; Isao Aoki, Muirfield, 1980; Greg Norman, Turnberry, 1986; Paul Broadhurst, St. Andrews, 1990; and Jodie Mudd, Royal Birkdale, 1991
7. Nick Faldo, 130 and 199, Muirfield, 1992
8. 267, Greg Norman, Royal St. George's, 1993
9. Jamie Anderson (1877-79), Robert Ferguson (1880-82) and Peter Thomson (1954-56)
10. Bobby Jones (1926-27), Walter Hagen (1928-29), Arnold Palmer (1961-62), Lee Trevino (1971-72) and Tom Watson (1982-83)
11. Willie Park, Sr. won in 1860 and Tom Morris, Sr in 1867. Tom Morris, Jr. won in 1868 and Willie Park, Jr. won in 1887.
12. Tom Morris, Jr., 17, 1868; Tom Morris, Sr., , 46, 1867
13. Bobby Jones, 1926. He won again as an amateur in 1927 and 1930.
14. John Daly, in a playoff at St. Andrews, 282, -6
15. A 4-hole medal play (total strokes) and sudden death if still tied

Jack the Bear

1. Jack Nicklaus has won the most major tournaments. How many?

2. Jack Nicklaus won the British Open three times, in 1966, '70, and '78. How many times did he finish second?

3. How many times did Jack win the U.S. Open?

4. How many Masters?

5. How many PGA's?

Jack the Bear

6. What other two "major" titles did he win?

7. Jack holds the record for being the tour's leading money winner the most years. How many years did he lead the tour?

8. How much total prize money did Jack Nicklaus win on the PGA Tour?

9. How much has he won on the Senior Tour?

10. What golf trophy has Jack Nicklaus never won?

Jack the Bear

11. Jack holds the Senior Tour 72-hole scoring record. What is it and where did he shoot it?

12. Jack had the largest 54-hole lead in a Senior event. What was it?

13. In what year and at what age did Jack turn pro?

14. Nicklaus leads the PGA tour in years on the Top 10 money list? How many?

15. Jack holds the PGA record for the most birdies in a row to win. What is it?

Jack the Bear

Answers

1. 18
2. 7 times, in 1964, '67, '68, '72, '76, '77, & '79
3. 4, 1962, '67, '72, '80
4. 6, 1963, '65, '66, '72, '75, '86
5. 5, 1963, '71, '73, '75, '80
6. Two U.S. Amateur Championships in 1959 and 1961
7. 8 times, 1964-'65, '67, '71-'73, '75-'76
8. $5,372,176 as of January 1, 1995
9. $1,243,588
10. The Vardon Trophy for lowest scoring average
11. 261 at the 1990 Mazda TPC
12. 8 strokes at the 1991 PGA Seniors Championship
13. In 1961 at the age of 21
14. 18 years
15. 5 at the 1978 Jackie Gleason Inverrary Classic

What's the Score?

1. Who holds the PGA record for the lowest 9-hole score ever shot in a PGA tour event?

2. What is the PGA tour event 18-hole PGA scoring record? Who holds it?

3. What is the 36-hole scoring record?

4. What's the lowest 54-hole total ever shot in a PGA tour event?

What's the Score?

5. Who holds the record for the lowest 72-hole total score?

6. What is the most shots under par ever shot in a 72-hole PGA tour event?

7. What is the record for the largest margin of victory in a PGA tour event?

8. Who holds the record for scoring the most consecutive birdies in a PGA tour event?

What's the Score?

9. Who holds the record for most birdies in a row to win a tournament?

10. What are the fewest putts taken in an 18-hole round in a PGA tour event?

11. What are the fewest putts taken in a 72-hole PGA tour event?

What's the Score?

Answers

1. 27 by Mike Souchak, in 1955, Texas Open; and Andy North in 1975, the B.C. Open

2. 59's, Al Geiberger in 1977, 2nd round, Memphis Danny Thomas Classic; and Chip Beck in 1991, 3rd round, the Las Vegas Invitational

3. 125, Ron Streck, 3rd and 4th rounds, 1988 Texas Open and Blaine McCallister, 2nd and 3rd rounds, 1988 Hardee's Golf Classic

4. 189, by Chandler Harper, 2nd, 3rd and 4th round, 1954 Texas Open

5. Mike Souchak (257), 1955 Texas Open

6. 27 under, Bobby Locke, 1948 Chicago Victory National

7. 16 strokes, by Ben Hogan, Portland Invitational, 1945, and Mike Souchak, 1955 Texas Open

8. 8, by Bob Goalby, 4th round, 1961 St. Petersburg Open; Fuzzy Zoeller, 1st round, 1976 Quad Cities Open; and Dewey Arnette, 1st round, 1987 Buick Open

9. 5, by Jack Nicklaus to win the 1978 Inverrary Classic

10. 18, Sam Trahan IV, 4th round of the 1979 Philadelphia Golf Classic; Mike McGee, 1st round, 1987 Federal Express St. Jude Classic; Kenny Knox, 1st round, 1989 MCI Heritage Classic; and Andy North, 2nd round, 1990 Anheuser Busch Classic

11. 93, by Kenny Knox, 1989 MCI Heritage Classic

Famous Firsts

1. Who is the first and only player to win the U.S. Open three consecutive times?

2. Who was the first of four men to win all four major tournaments in his career?

3. Who was the first player to break the $100,000 mark in one-year PGA earnings?

4. What distinction is held by Bob Charles for his victory over Phil Rodgers in the 1963 British Open?

5. When was the first playoff in the U.S.?

Famous Firsts

6. When was the first major tournament decided in a sudden-death playoff?

7. Which major was first to change from a 18-hole playoff format to sudden-death?

8. What was the first nationally televised golf tournament?

9. What was Bobby Jones' first notable golf appearance?

10. Who was the first player to use a "sand wedge" in tournament play?

Famous Firsts

11. What is significant about Fuzzy Zoeller's first appearance in The Masters in 1979?

12. In 1962, what PGA Tour rookie claimed the U.S. Open as his very first victory?

13. The U.S. Open has been first tour victory for two other Tour rookies. Who are they?

14. What tour rookie won a PGA Championship as his first victory?

15. The youngest player to win the U. S. Amateur is also the first and only black U.S. Amateur champion. Who is he?

Famous Firsts

Answers

1. Willie Anderson, 1903-05

2. Gene Sarazen completed the slam with The Masters in 1935. The other three are Jack Nicklaus, Gary Player & Ben Hogan.

3. Arnold Palmer, 1963

4. He became the first left-hander to win a major.

5. 1901 at the Myopia Hunt Club between Willie Anderson and Alex Smith. Anderson beat Smith (85-86) in the 18-hole play-off.

6. The 1967 PGA at Pebble Beach. Lanny Wadkins beat Gene Littler in three holes.

7. The Masters, in 1976

8. The 1953 World Championship of Golf. Lew Worsham holed his second shot for an eagle on the 18th hole to win by one shot over Chandler Harper.

9. He played in the 1916 U.S. Amateur at the age of 14.

10. Gene Sarazen introduced the club when he won the 1932 British Open.

11. He won it.

12. Jack Nicklaus

13. Jerry Pate, in 1976, and Ernie Els in 1994

14. John Daly, in 1991

15. Tiger Woods, in 1994, at the age of 18

The Masters

1. Who won the first Masters?

2. What two players have won back-to-back Masters?

3. Who shot the lowest single round score for any Masters?

4. What two players hold the record for the lowest 72-hole total in The Masters?

5. Who is the oldest player to win The Masters?

The Masters

6. Who was the youngest?

7. What four legendary golfers each won The Masters two or more times before 1955?

8. What was the largest winning margin in The Masters?

9. How long is the Augusta National course?

10. Besides prize money, what is awarded to the winner of The Masters?

The Masters

11. What amateurs are invited to play in The Masters?

12. What is the highest single hole score in Masters competition?

13. Three players have made double eagles at The Masters. Can you name them?

14. Who won and who lost the 1968 Masters due to the signing of an incorrect scorecard?

15. Who won the 1995 Masters and the death of what legendary teacher might have been the inspiration for his victory?

The Masters

Answers

1. Horton Smith, 1934, Augusta National Golf Course in Augusta, Georgia. He also won in 1936.
2. Jack Nicklaus, 1965-66, and Nick Faldo, 1989-90
3. Nick Price shot 63 in the 1986 Masters.
4. Jack Nicklaus (1965) and Ray Floyd (1976) had 271 Masters totals.
5. Jack Nicklaus was 46 in 1986.
6. Seve Ballesteros was 23 in 1980.
7. Jimmy Demaret (1940, '47, '50), Sam Snead (1949, '52, '54), Byron Nelson (1937, '42) and Ben Hogan (1951, '53)
8. Jack Nicklaus won the 1965 Masters by a 9-stroke margin.
9. 6,980 yds.
10. The green jacket
11. The most recent U.S. Amateur winner and runner-up, winners of the U.S. Mid-Amateur, the U.S. Public Links, and the British Amateur
12. Tommy Nakajima, 13 on the par-5 13th hole in 1978 and Tom Weiskopf, 13 on the par-3 12th hole in 1980
13. Gene Sarazen holed a 4-wood at the 15th in 1935, Bruce Devlin holed a 4-wood at the 8th in 1967, and Jeff Maggert made two on the 13th with a 3-iron in 1994.
14. Bob Goalby, Roberto de Vicenzo
15. Ben Crenshaw shot -14, 274, Harvey Penick

The Foreign Brigade

1. What South African has won the British Open three times?

2. How many times has Seve Ballesteros won the British Open?

3. What British player has won the British Open three times since 1985?

4. One other foreign player has won it twice since then. Who is he?

5. Who was the 1994 U.S. Open champion and what country does he represent?

The Foreign Brigade

6. What German player has won The Masters twice?

7. What Spanish players have won The Masters?

8. How many Masters has Gary Player won?

9. For six out the last eight years foreign players have won this PGA major tournament. What is it and who are they?

10. Since 1979, foreign born players have won this major 11 times. What is it and who are they?

The Foreign Brigade

11. What player on the U.S. tour represents the island of Fiji?

12. Who are the best known Japanese players on the regular and Senior PGA Tour?

13. What Scandinavian player finished second in the 1994 British Open and is probably better known for playing with the bill of his cap flipped up?

14. What Italian player finished second in the 1995 British Open?

15. What country does Steve Elkington, 1995 PGA champion, represent?

The Foreign Brigade

Answers

1. Gary Player (1959, '68, '74)

2. Three times (1979, '84, '88)

3. Nick Faldo (1987, '90, '92)

4. Greg Norman (1986, '93)

5. Ernie Els, South Africa

6. Bernhard Langer, 1985 and '93

7. Seve Ballesteros, 1980 and '83, and Jose Maria Olazabel, 1994

8. Three, 1961, '74, and '78

9. The Masters, Olazabel (1994), Langer (1993), Ian Woosnam (1991), Faldo ('89 and '90), and Sandy Lyle (1988)

10. The British Open, Nick Price (1994), Norman ('86 and '93), Faldo ('87, 90, and '92), Ian Baker-Finch (1991), Lyle (1985) and Ballesteros ('79, '84, and '88).

11. Vijay Singh

12. Jumbo Ozaki and Isao Aoki

13. Jesper Parnevik

14. Constantino Rocca lost a 4-hole playoff to John Daly.

15. Australia

Arnie's Army

1. How many times has Arnold Palmer won the British Open?

2. How many times has he won The Masters?

3. Arnold Palmer won the U.S. Open one time, in 1960. How many times did he finish second?

4. In what years was Arnold Palmer the PGA Tour's leading money winner?

5. How many consecutive years was Arnie in the Top 10 money list?

Arnie's Army

6. How much total prize money did Arnold Palmer win on the PGA Tour?

7. How much has he won on the Senior Tour?

8. In what year did Arnold Palmer play his last U.S. Open?

9. What major regular Tour tournament did Arnold Palmer fail to win?

10. How many times did he finish second in that tournament?

Arnie's Army

11. Arnold Palmer was the first PGA player to win $1,000,000 in his career. When did he do it?

12. Arnie shares the record with Jack Nicklaus for the most consecutive years on the tour with at least one victory. How many?

13. In what year did Arnold turn pro?

14. Arnold is tied with Orville Moody for the largest winning margin in a Senior Tour event. What is it?

15. In what year did Arnie play his final British Open?

Arnie's Army

Answers

1. Two times (1961, '62)

2. Four times, 1958, '60, '62, and '64

3. Four times, 1962, '63, '66' and '67

4. 1958 ($42,407), '60 ($75,262), '62 ($81,448) and '63 ($128,230)

5. 15

6. $1,904,667

7. $1,500,776+

8. 1994

9. The PGA

10. Three, '64, '68, and '70

11. At the 1968 PGA Classic, Arnold won $12,500 for finishing 2nd. He surpassed a million after 13 years on the Tour.

12. 17

13. 1954, when he was 25

14. 11 strokes. Arnie did it in 1985 at the Senior TPC, and Orville did it in 1988 at the Vintage Chrysler Invitational.

15. 1995, at St. Andrews

PGA Potpourri

1. What is the PGA Tour's Grand Slam?

2. What golfer has come the closest to winning the Grand Slam in the same year?

3. What four major titles (that at one time constituted the Grand Slam) did Bobby Jones win in the same year?

4. Who holds the record for having the most wins in one single event?

5. Who holds the record for the most tournaments won in one year?

PGA Potpourri

6. Who has won the most PGA tournaments in his career?

7. Who is the oldest person to have won a regular PGA tour event?

8. What's the most money ever won on the PGA tour in one year by one player?

9. What is the Vardon Trophy and who was Harry Vardon?

10. The 1994 Vardon Trophy winner won with a record scoring average. Who was he and what was his average?

PGA Potpourri

11. Two players have won the Vardon Trophy 5 times each. Who are they?

12. What PGA players have each won three NCAA titles?

13. What PGA Tour players have won both NCAA and U.S. Amateur titles?

14. How long has it been since Americans won the Grand Slam, all four majors, in one year?

PGA Potpourri

Answers

1. The Masters, the U.S. Open, the British Open, and the PGA
2. Ben Hogan, 1951, The Masters, the U.S. Open, and the British Open
3. The U.S. and British Opens and the U.S. and British Amateur Championships, in 1930
4. Sam Snead, 8 Greater Greensboro Opens, 1938, '46, '49-'50, '55-'56, '60 and '65
5. Byron Nelson, 18 events in 1945, including 11 straight
6. Sam Snead, 84
7. Sam Snead, 52 years and 10 months, 1965 Greater Greensboro Open
8. As of the 1995 World Series of Golf, $1,555,709 by Greg Norman
9. The title for the lowest average score per 18 holes on the PGA Tour in honor of an Englishman, Harry Vardon
10. Greg Norman, 68.81
11. Billy Casper and Lee Trevino
12. Ben Crenshaw, 1971-73, University of Texas; Phil Mickelson in 1989-90 and 1992 for Arizona State
13. Jack Nicklaus (NCAA, 1961, U.S. Amateur, 1959 and 61), Scott Verplank (NCAA, 1986, U.S. Amateur, 1984), and Mickelson (U.S. Amateur, 1990)
14. 1982. Tom Watson won the British and U.S. Opens, Craig Stadler won the Masters, and Raymond Floyd won the PGA.

The U.S. Open

1. When and where was the first U.S. Open played and who won?

2. Who has won the most U.S. Opens?

3. Who shot the lowest single round score for any U.S. Open?

4. Who holds the record for the lowest 72-hole total in the U.S. Open?

5. Who is the oldest player to win the U.S. Open?

The U.S. Open

6. Who was the youngest?

7. What was the largest winning margin in U.S. Open history?

8. Who were the three players in the playoff for the 1994 Open title?

9. What is the U.S. Open playoff format?

10. Since 1970, the U.S. Open has been won 7 times in playoffs. Who were the playoff winners?

The U.S. Open

11. The longest playoff in major tournament history occurred in a U.S. Open. When was it?

12. How many times in the 94-year U.S. Open history has the championship been decided in a playoff?

13. Who won the 1995 U.S Open?

The U.S. Open

Answers

1. Horace Rawlins, in 1895, at Newport Golf Club, Newport, R.I.

2. Willie Anderson, 1901, '03, '04, '05; Bobby Jones, 1923, '26, '29, '30; Ben Hogan, 1948, '50, '51, '53; and Jack Nicklaus, 1962, '67, '72, '80.

3. 63, Johnny Miller, Oakmont, 1973 and Jack Nicklaus and Tom Weiskopf on the same day at Baltusrol in 1980

4. Jack Nicklaus, 272 (63, 71, 70, 68), Baltusrol, 1980; and Lee Janzen, Baltusrol, 1993

5. Hale Irwin, 45, 1990 for the third time (1974, '79, '90)

6. John McDermott, 19, in 1911

7. Willie Smith, 11 strokes in 1899

8. Colin Montgomerie of Great Britain and Loren Roberts of the USA lost to Ernie Els of South Africa.

9. 18-hole playoff

10. Lee Trevino (1971), Lou Graham (1975), Fuzzy Zoeller (1984), Curtis Strange (1988), Hale Irwin (1990), Payne Stewart (1991), and Ernie Els (1994)

11. In the 1931 U.S. Open, Billy Burke beat George Von Elm by one shot after two 36 hole playoffs. The Open returned to an 18-hole playoff format in 1932.

12. 31

13. Corey Pavin shot even par 280 at Shinnecock.

How Many's

1. How many regular PGA Tour majors has Raymond Floyd won?

2. How many majors did Gary Player win on the regular PGA Tour?

3. How many majors has Tom Watson won?

4. How many consecutive years did Jack Nicklaus and Arnold Palmer have at least one tour victory.

5. How many Vardon trophies does Tom Watson have?

How Many's

6. How many consecutive years did John Daly lead the Tour in driving distance?

7. Since 1980, who has led the Tour in driving accuracy for the most consecutive years?

8. Since 1980, what pro holds the record for the number of eagles scored in one tour season?

9. What is the record for most birdies in one tour season since 1980?

10. Who holds the record for consecutive years at the top of the Top 10 Money List?

How Many's

11. Chi Chi Rodriguez holds the record for the most consecutive birdies in a Senior Tour event. What is it?

12. Chi Chi also holds the record for the most consecutive victories on the Senior Tour. How many?

13. How many players participated in the largest sudden death playoff?

14. What is the record for the most victories in a calendar year on the regular PGA Tour?

15. What is the PGA record for the most consecutive victories in a single event?

How Many's

Answers

1. Four, 2 PGA's (1969, '82), the 1986 U.S. Open, and the 1976 Masters

2. Nine, 3 British Opens ('59, '68, '74), 3 Masters ('61, '74, '78), 2 PGA's ('62, '72) and the 1965 U.S. Open

3. Eight, 5 British Opens ('75, '77, '80, 82, & 83), 2 Masters ('77 & '81), and one U.S. Open (1982)

4. 17, Nicklaus, 1962-'78, Palmer, 1955-'71

5. Three, 1977-'79

6. Three, 1991-'93

7. Calvin Peete led 10 consecutive years, from 1981 to 1990.

8. Ken Green made 21 in 1988.

9. 465 by Dan Forsman in 1988

10. Tom Watson 1977-'80

11. 8 in a row at the 1987 Silver Pages Classic

12. He won 4 in a row in 1987.

13. There were 6 in the 1994 GTE Byron Nelson Classic.

14. Byron Nelson won 18 in 1945.

15. Walter Hagen won the PGA Championship 4 straight times, from 1924 to 1927.

The Merry Mex

1. How many times has Lee Trevino won the British Open?

2. How many times has he won the U.S. Open?

3. In each of Lee's U.S. Open victories, who was the runner-up?

4. What major tournament did Lee Trevino never win?

5. What odd thing happened to Lee at the 1976 Western Open?

The Merry Mex

6. What were Lee's total money winnings on the PGA Tour?

7. How many times has Lee Trevino won the Senior U.S. Open?

8. How much money has he won on the Senior Tour?

9. Lee won what two distinctions in 1990 on the Senior Tour?

10. What other two Senior PGA Tour records did Lee set in 1990?

The Merry Mex

11. In what year did Lee on the Senior Tour outearn Greg Norman, the leader on the regular PGA tour?

12. Lee is ranked number one in all-time Senior Tour wins. How many?

13. In what year did Lee turn pro?

14. Lee set the Senior tour record for most consecutive sub-70 rounds. In what year and how many?

15. Lee also holds the record for the most consecutive par-or-less rounds. What is it and when did he do it?

The Merry Mex

Answers

1. Two times (1971, '72)

2. Twice (1968, '71)

3. Jack Nicklaus

4. The Masters

5. He was struck by lightning.

6. $3,478,449

7. Once, 1990

8. $5,108,902, through 1994

9. He won Rookie of the Year and Player of the Year honors.

10. Best all-time scoring average (68.89) and most money won by a first year player, $1,190,518

11. In 1990, $1,190,518 to $1,165,477

12. 25

13. 1960, at the age of 21

14. In 1992, he had 11.

15. 27, in 1992

The Playoffs

1. What player has won both of his major tournaments in playoffs?

2. What Tour player has the worst playoff record?

3. Two players have each lost all four majors in playoffs. Who are they?

4. What four players have defeated the same player in playoffs to win major championships?

5. What is said to be the worst defeat in playoff history?

The Playoffs

Answers

1. Fuzzy Zoeller beat Tom Watson and Ed Sneed in the 1979 Masters and Greg Norman in the 1984 U.S. Open.

2. Ben Crenshaw is 0-8.

3. Craig Wood (1933 British Open, 1934 PGA, 1935 Masters, and the 1939 U.S. Open) and Greg Norman (1984 Open, 1987 Masters, the 1989 British Open, and the 1993 PGA).

4. Fuzzy Zoeller ('84 Open), Larry Mize ('87 Masters), Mark Calchavecchia ('89 British), and Paul Azinger ('93 PGA) all defeated Norman.

5. Bobby Jones beat Al Espinosa by 23 strokes in a 36-hole playoff at the 1929 U.S. Open.

The PGA Championship

1. What does PGA stand for?

2. When was the first PGA Championship played and who won?

3. What two players are tied for having won the most PGA titles?

4. Who has won the most consecutive PGA championships?

5. Three players have each won the PGA twice since 1974. Who are they?

The PGA Championship

6. What five modern-day legendary golfers have never won the PGA title?

7. What PGA rookie won the title in 1991?

8. What is the single-round scoring record for the PGA?

9. Who holds the record for the lowest 72-hole total in the PGA?

10. Who were the oldest and youngest players to win the PGA?

The PGA Championship

11. How many times has the PGA been won in a play-off prior to 1995?

12. Who lost the playoff in 1993?

13. Who are only two players to win the British Open and the PGA Championship in the same year?

14. Who won the 1995 PGA Championship and what record did he set?

The PGA Championship

Answers

1. Professional Golfers Association
2. 1916, Jim Barnes, Siwanoy Country Club, Bronxville, N.Y.
3. Walter Hagen (5, 1921, 1924-27) and Jack Nicklaus (5, 1963, '71, '73, '75 and '80)
4. Walter Hagen won it 4 consecutive times (1924-27).
5. Lee Trevino (1974, '84), Larry Nelson (1981, '87) and Nicklaus (1975, '80)
6. Arnold Palmer, Tom Watson, Hale Irwin, Nick Faldo and Greg Norman
7. John Daly
8. 63, by Bruce Crampton (1975) at Firestone, Ray Floyd (1982) at Southern Hills, and a host of others in 1995
9. Steve Elkington and Colin Montgomerie, 267, in 1995
10. Julius Boros, 48 in 1968; Gene Sarazen, 20, in 1922
11. 5 times, by Jerry Barber in 1961, Don January in 1967, Lanny Wadkins in 1977, David Graham in 1979, and Paul Azinger in 1993
12. Greg Norman
13. Walter Hagen, 1924, and Nick Price, 1994
14. Steve Elkington shot 64 at Riviera Country Club, the lowest final round to win in a PGA Championship, and won on the first hole of a sudden death playoff with Colin Montgomerie.

The LPGA

The LPGA U. S. Open

1. Who won the the first Women's U.S. Open played?

2. What distinction does the first LPGA U.S. Open have?

3. Who has won the most LPGA U.S. Opens?

4. What players have won back-to-back LPGA U.S. Open titles?

5. Who shot the lowest single round score for any Women's U.S. Open?

The LPGA U. S. Open

6. Who holds the record for the lowest 72-hole total in the Women's U.S. Open?

7. Who is the oldest player to win the LPGA U.S. Open?

8. Who was the youngest?

9. What was the largest winning margin in LPGA U.S. Open history?

10. Who was the 1995 LPGA U.S. Open champion?

The LPGA U. S. Open

11. Who came in second?

12. What is the LPGA U.S. Open playoff format?

13. How many times has the Women's U.S. Open been won in playoffs?

14. Two LPGA players have each been runner-up in the U.S. Open five times. Who are they?

The LPGA U. S. Open

Answers

1. Patty Berg in 1946

2. It was the only match play Women's U.S. Open.

3. Betsy Rawls (1951, '53, '57, '60) and Mickey Wright (1958-59, '61, and '64) won it four times each.

4. Five players have won it consecutively: Mickey Wright (1958-59), Donna Caponi Young (1969-70), Susie Berning (1972-73), Hollis Stacy (1977-78), and Betsy King (1989-90).

5. 65 by Sallie Little in the 4th round in 1978 and Judy Dickinson in the third round in 1985

6. Pat Bradley had a 279 total in 1981.

7. Fay Crocker was 40 in 1955.

8. Catherine Lacoste was 22 in 1967.

9. 14 strokes by Louise Suggs in 1949

10. Annika Sorenstam, -2, 278

11. Meg Mallon, who led Sorenstam by 5 shots after 54 holes

12. Up until 1992, it was 18-hole format.

13. 7 times, ('53,'56,'64,'76,'86,'87,'92)

14. Louise Suggs ('51,'55,'58,'59,'63) & Joanne Carner ('75,'78,'82,'83,'87)

LPGA Championship

1. When was the LPGA formed?

2. What was it known as before 1950?

3. Who won the first LPGA Championship?

4. Who has won the most LPGA Championships?

5. What players have won back-to-back LPGA titles?

LPGA Championship

6. What is the single-round scoring record for the LPGA Championship?

7. Who holds the record for the lowest 72-hole total in the LPGA Championship?

8. 1994 marked the first time the LPGA Championship was played on this course? What is it?

9. Who won the 1995 McDonalds LPGA Championship?

LPGA Championship

10. Who was the runner-up?

11. Who has the most runner-up finishes in this tournament?

12. Two players have each finished second three times. Who are they?

13. Besides Mickey Wright, two other players have each won this tournament three times. Who are they?

LPGA Championship

Answers

1. The LPGA was chartered in 1950.

2. The WWGA

3. Beverly Hanson, in 1955, at Orchard Ridge in Fort Wayne, Indiana

4. Mickey Wright won four times (1958, '60, '61, '63)

5. Mickey Wright (1960-61) and Patty Sheehan (1983-84)

6. 63 by Patty Sheehan in 1984

7. Betsy King had a 267 total (-17) at Bethesda in 1992.

8. The DuPont Country Club in Wilmington, Delaware

9. Kelly Robbins, -10, 274

10. Laura Davies

11. Louise Suggs, 4 times

12. Pat Bradley ('77,'84,'91) and Joanne Carner ('74,'82,'92)

13. Kathy Whitworth ('67,'71,'75) and Patty Sheehan ('83,'84,'93)

The Dinah Shore

1. Who won the first Dinah Shore championship?

2. Who has won the most Dinah Shore Championships?

3. What is the single-round scoring record for the Dinah Shore?

4. What is the record for the lowest 72-hole total in the Colgate/Nabisco Dinah Shore?

5. Who won the 1995 Dinah Shore?

The Dinah Shore

Answers
1. Jane Blaylock in 1972 at Mission Hills Country Club in Rancho Mirage, CA
2. Amy Alcott has won three times, 1983, '88 and '91.
3. Nancy Lopez shot 64 in 1981.
4. 273 by Amy Alcott in 1991
5. Nanci Bowen, 3 under par 285

The Du Maurier Limited Classic

1. Who won the first Du Maurier Classic?

2. What player has won the most Du Maurier tournaments?

3. What is the single-round scoring record for the Du Maurier Classic?

4. Who holds the record for the lowest 72-hole total in the Du Maurier Classic?

5. Who won it in 1995?

The Du Maurier Limited Classic

Answers
1. Jocelyne Bourassa, in 1973 at the Royal Montreal Golf Club, Montreal, Canada
2. Pat Bradley has won three times, 1980, '85 and '86.
3. 64 by Joanne Carner in 1978
4. Pat Bradley, Ayako Okamoto, and Cathy Johnson have shot 276.
5. Jenny Lidback shot an 8-under 280 for her first LPGA tour victory.

LPGA Potpourri

1. Who holds the record for the most Rolex Player of the Year awards?

2. Who was the 1995 Rolex LPGA Player of the Year?

3. What is the Vare trophy?

4. Who has won the most Vare Trophies?

5. Who was the 1995 Vare Trophy winner?

LPGA Potpourri

6. Two players hold the record for the lowest 72-hole score in a LPGA event? Who are they?

7. Four players are tied for the lowest 18-hole scoring LPGA scoring record? Who are they?

8. What is the largest winning margin in the history of the LPGA?

9. Who holds the record for the most consecutive birdies in a LPGA tournament?

10. Who has the most holes-in-one on the LPGA tour?

LPGA Potpourri

11. Who holds the LPGA record for the most holes-in-one in a tournament?

12. What LPGA player has the most eagles in one round?

13. Who holds the record for the most sub-par holes in a single LPGA event?

14. Who holds the record for the most rounds in the 60's in a calendar year?

15. Who has the most career victories on the LPGA tour?

LPGA Potpourri

Answers

1. Kathy Whitworth with seven
2. Annika Sorenstam.
3. The LPGA award for the lowest annual scoring average
4. Kathy Whitworth has won seven.
5. Annika Sorenstam.
6. 268, Nancy Lopez, Willow Creek, 1985, and Beth Daniel, Walnut Hills, 1994
7. 62, Mickey Wright, 1964 Tall City Open; Vicki Fergon, 1984 San Jose Classic; Laura Davies, 1991 Rail Charity Golf Classic; and Hollis Stacy, 1992 Safeco Classic
8. 14 shots, Louise Suggs, 1949 U.S. Women's Open, and Cindy Mackey, 1986 Mastercard International Pro Am
9. 8, Mary Beth Zimmerman in the 1984 Rail Charity Golf Classic
10. Kathy Whitworth has had 11 holes-in-one.
11. 2, Jo Ann Washam, 1979 Women Kemper Open
12. Alice Ritzman made 3 eagles in the 1979 Colgate European Open.
13. 1985 Henredon Classic, Nancy Lopez, 25 of the 72 holes under par.
14. 33 by Betsy King in 1989
15. Kathy Whitworth with 88 wins

The Seniors

The Majors

1. What Senior PGA events constitute the four majors?

2. What is the oldest and longest running of the Senior majors?

3. Where was it first held and who won?

4. Who has won the most PGA Seniors titles?

5. Who holds the PGA Seniors 72-hole scoring record?

The Majors

6. When and where was The Tradition first held and who won?

7. What is The Traditon 72-hole tournament scoring record?

8. When was the first Senior Players Championship held and who won?

9. Who is the only player to win back-to-back Senior Players titles?

10. What is the Senior Players Championship tournament 72-hole scoring record?

The Majors

11. Who won the first Senior U.S. Open played?

12. Who has won the most Senior U.S. Opens?

13. Who are the only players to win it consecutive times?

14. Who shot the lowest 72-hole score for U.S. Senior Open?

15. Who were the 1995 Senior majors winners?

The Majors

Answers

1. The Tradition, The PGA Seniors, The U.S. Senior Open, and the Senior Players Championship
2. The PGA Seniors Championship began in 1937.
3. At Augusta National and won by Jock Hutchinson
4. Sam Snead, six times, in 1964-65, '67, '70, and '72-73
5. Jack Nicklaus, 17 under par 271, in 1991
6. 1989 at the Cochise Course, Desert Mountain Golf Club in Scottsdale AZ, won by Don Bies
7. Lee Trevino, 14 under par 274, in 1992
8. 1983, Miller Barber
9. Arnold Palmer, 1984-'85
10. 27 under par 261 by Jack Nicklaus in 1990
11. Roberto DeVicenzo, 1980, Winged Foot Golf Club, N.Y.
12. Miller Barber, 3, 1982, '84 and '85
13. Barber, '84-85, and Gary Player, '87-88
14. Gary Player, in 1987, with a 270 total
15. Jack Nicklaus (The Tradition), Tom Weiskopf (U.S. Senior Open), Raymond Floyd (PGA Seniors), and J.C. Snead (Senior Players Championship)

The Skins Games

1. What is a "skins" game?

2. When and where was the first PGA skins game?

3. Who were the four participants in the first PGA Skins Game and who won?

4. Who has won the most money in one PGA Skins event?

5. What PGA Skins player has won the most total $$$ in the Skins games?

The Skins Games

6. Who played in and who won the 1995 PGA Skins game?

7. In the 1995 Skins game the most money ever won on one hole took place. Who won and how much?

8. The first Senior Skins Game took place where and who won?

9. What players have played in both regular tour Skins games and Senior Skins games?

The Skins Games

10. What senior tour player has won the most money in a single Senior Skins game?

11. What senior has won the most total money in Senior Skins games?

12. What players have won both regular tour and Senior Skins games?

13. When was the first LPGA Skins game and who won?

14. Who won the 1995 LPGA Skins game?

The Skins Games

Answers

1. A match play game where the best ball of a foursome wins a designated amount of money on each hole. If no one wins the hole, it's value is "carried over" and added on to the value of the next hole.

2. 1983, at Desert Highlands Country Club in Scottsdale, Arizona. Gary Player won $170,000.

3. Arnold Palmer, Jack Nicklaus, Gary Player, and Lee Trevino

4. Fuzzy Zoeller won $370,000 in 1986.

5. Fred Couples has won $910,000, 1992-1995.

6. Fred Couples won. His partners were Corey Pavin, Peter Jacobsen and 1994 defending champ Tom Watson.

7. Couples won only one skin worth $270,000 on the fifth sudden death hole.

8. Chi Chi Rodriguez won $300,000 at Turtle Bay Golf Club, Oahu, Hawaii in 1988.

9. Arnold Palmer, Lee Trevino, Jack Nicklaus, and Raymond Floyd

10. Jack Nicklaus won $310,000 in 1991.

11. Arnold Palmer has won $635,000, winning in 1990, 1992-93.

12. Jack Nicklaus and Raymond Floyd

13. In 1990, Jan Stephenson won $200,000.

14. Dottie Mochrie

1995 PGA Senior Tour

Senior Money Leaders

Match the Senior Tour player with his 1995 money earnings.

1. $1,444,386   a. Ray Floyd
2. $1,419,545   b. Lee Trevino
3. $1,415,847   c. Jim Colbert
4. $1,241,524   d. Dave Stockton
5. $1,041,766   e. Hale Irwin
6. $978,137   f. Isao Aoki
7. $943,993   g. J C. Snead
8. $849,350   h. Bob Murphy
9. $844,687   i. Tom Wargo
10. $799,175   j. Graham Marsh

Senior Money Leaders

Answers
1. c. Jim Colbert
2. a. Ray Floyd
3. d. Dave Stockton
4. h. Bob Murphy
5. f. Isao Aoki
6. g. J C. Snead
7. b. Lee Trevino
8. j. Graham Marsh
9. i. Tom Wargo
10. e. Hale Irwin

PGA Senior All-Time Old Money

Match the PGA Senior Tour player with his rank and winnings as of January 1, 1996 on the all-time Senior earnings list.

1. $5,784,327   a. Chi Chi Rodriguez

2. $5,640,898   b. George Archer

3. $5,244,386   c. Bob Charles

4. $4,994,635   d. Lee Trevino

5. $4,967,092   e. Mike Hill

PGA Senior All-Time Old Money

Answers
1. d
2. c
3. a
4. e
5. b

1990s Old Money Match

Match the Senior Tour players with their 1990's earnings as of January 1, 1996.

1. $6,043,636   a. Jim Colbert

2. $5,006,110   b. Bob Charles

3. $4,942,907   c. George Archer

4. $4,718,031   d. Lee Trevino

5. $3,950,614   e. Mike Hill

1990s Old Money Match

Answers
1. d
2. c
3. a
4. e
5. b

Senior Scoring Leaders

Match the Senior Tour player with his average 18-hole score in 1995.

1. 69.30
2. 69.38
3. 69.47
4. 69.59
5. 69.67
6. 69.76
7. 69.85
8. 69.87
9. 69.99
10. 70.03

a. Lee Trevino
b. Ray Floyd
c. Dave Stockton
d. Isao Aoki
e. Bob Murphy
f. Don January
g. Gay Brewer
h. Dick Rhyan
i. Joe Jimenez
j. Jim Ferree

Senior Scoring Leaders

Answers
1. j. Jim Ferree
2. h. Dick Rhyan
3. b. Ray Floyd
4. i. Joe Jimenez
5. d. Isao Aoki
6. f. Don January
7. c. Dave Stockton
8. e. Bob Murphy
9. g. Gay Brewer
10. a. Lee Trevino

Senior Putting Leaders

Match the Senior Tour player with his average putts per hole in 1995.

1. 1.738   a. Ray Floyd

2. 1.743   b. Lee Trevino

3. 1.744   c. Graham Marsh

4. (tie) 1.753   d. Isao Aoki

4. (tie)   e. Dave Stockton

Senior Putting Leaders

Answers
 1. d. Isao Aoki
 2. b. Lee Trevino
 3. e. Dave Stockton
 4. a. Ray Floyd
 4. c. Graham Marsh

Senior Stat Leaders

Match the Senior Tour player with the statistical category he led in 1995.

1. Eagle Leader

a. Ray Floyd

2. Greens in Regulation

b. Dave Stockton

3. Driving Accuracy

c. Dave Eichelberger

4. Sand Saves

d. Deane Beman

5. Birdie Leader

e. Bruce Summerhays

Senior Stat Leaders

Answers
1. c. Dave Eichelberger (13)
2. a. Ray Floyd (75.3)
3. d. Deane Beman (80.6)
4. b. Dave Stockton (57.8)
5. e. Bruce Summerhays (411)

1995 Senior PGA Driving Distance

Match the Senior Tour player with his 1995 average driving distance.

1. 277.4   a. Jim Dent

2. 273.9   b. Tom Weiskopf

3. 273.4   c. Ray Floyd

4. 272.8   d. Jay Sigel

5. 269.8   e. Terry Dill

6. 268.1   f. Dave Eichelberger

1995 Senior PGA Driving Distance

Answers
1. d. Jay Sigel
2. a. Jim Dent
3. e. Terry Dill
4. f. Dave Eichelberger
5. b. Tom Weiskopf
6. c. Ray Floyd

More Senior $$$$

Match these Senior Tour player with their 1995 money earnings and ranking on the money list.

1. Tom Weiskopf
2. George Archer
3. Bob Charles
4. Jim Albus
5. Jay Sigel
6. Jack Nicklaus
7. Jim Dent
8. Gary Player
9. Chi Chi Rodriguez
10. Arnold Palmer

a. $752,087 (11)
b. $744,936 (12)
c. $659,923 (15)
d. $580,137 (18)
e. $575,603 (19)
f. $51,526 (86)
g. $567,557 (21)
h. $538,800 (22)
i. $309,251 (38)
j. $194,922 (53)

More Senior $$$$

Answers
1. d. $580,137 (18)
2. a. $752,087 (11)
3. c. $659,923 (15)
4. b. $744,936 (12)
5. g. $567,557 (21)
6. h. $538,800 (22)
7. e. $575,603 (19)
8. i. $309,251 (38)
9. j. $194,922 (53)
10. f. $51,526 (86)

1995 LPGA

1995 LPGA Money Leaders Match

Match the LPGA player with her 1995 money winnings.

1. $666,533
2. $530,349
3. $527,655
4. $521,000
5. $481,149
6. $480,124
7. $449,296
8. $434,986
9. $430,248
10. $426,957

a. Laura Davies
b. Betsy King
c. Meg Mallon
d. Annika Sorenstam
e. Val Skinner
f. Dottie Mochrie
g. Kelly Robbins
h. Michelle McGann
i. Beth Daniel
j. Rosie Jones

1995 LPGA Money Leaders Match

Answers
1. d. Annika Sorenstam
2. a. Laura Davies
3. g. Kelly Robbins
4. f. Dottie Mochrie
5. b. Betsy King
6. i. Beth Daniel
7. h. Michelle McGann
8. c. Meg Mallon
9. e. Val Skinner
10. j. Rosie Jones

LPGA Career Earnings Match

Match the LPGA player with her career money winnings (as of January 1, 1996).

1. $5,374,022
2. $5,141,019
3. $4,972,215
4. $4,788,546
5. $4,275,684
6. $3,135,772
7. $3,095,716
8. $2,878,104
9. $2,735,629
10. $2,620,005

a. Nancy Lopez
b. Dottie Mochrie
c. Betsy King
d. Amy Alcott
e. Joanne Carner
f. Pat Bradley
g. Rosie Jones
h. Patty Sheehan
i. Ayako Okamoto
j. Beth Daniel

LPGA Career Earnings Match

Answers
1. c
2. f
3. j
4. h
5. a.
6. d
7. b
8. e
9. i
10. g

1995 LPGA Tour Winners

Match the LPGA player with the tournament she won in 1995.

1. LPGA Championship   a. Annika Sorenstam

2. Sprint Championship   b. Val Skinner

3. du Maurier Classic   c. Kelly Robbins

4. British Open   d. Nanci Bowen

5. US Women's Open   e. Jenny Lidback

6. Nabisco Dinah Shore   f. Karrie Webb

1995 LPGA Tour Winners

Answers
1. c. Kelly Robbins
2. b. Val Skinner
3. e. Jenny Lidback
4. f. Karrie Webb
5. a. Annika Sorenstam
6. d. Nanci Bowen

1995 LPGA Tournament $$$$

Match the 1995 LPGA Tournament with the winner's purse.

1. $180,000	a. du Maurier Classic
2. $175,000	b. Oldsmobile Classic
3. $150,000	c. Tournament of Champions
4. $127,500	d. US Women's Open
5. $117,500	e. Sara Lee Classic Championship
6. $115,000	f. Toray Japan Queens Cup
7. $105,000	g. LPGA Championship
8. $ 96,000	h. Samsung World
9. $ 90,000	i. British Open
10. $ 78,750	j. Nabisco Dinah Shore

1995 LPGA Tournament $$$$

Answers
1. g. LPGA Championship
2. d. US Women's Open
3. a. du Maurier Classic
4. j. Nabisco Dinah Shore
5. h. Samsung World Championship
6. c. Tournament of Champions
7. f. Toray Japan Queens Cup
8. i. British Open
9. b. Oldsmobile Classic
10. e. Sara Lee Classic

More 1995 Tournament Winners

Match these LPGA players with the 1995 tournament they won.

1. Tournament of Champions   a. Woo-Soon Ko

2. Toray Japan Queens Cup   b. Patty Sheehan

3. Safeco Classic   c. Dawn Coe-Jones

4. Standard Register/PING   d. Laura Davies

5. Sara Lee Classic   e. Beth Daniel

6. PING Welch's Championship   f. Michelle McGann

More 1995 Tournament Winners

Answers
1. c. Dawn Coe-Jones
2. a. Woo-Soon Ko
3. b. Patty Sheehan
4. d. Laura Davies
5. f. Michelle McGann
6. e. Beth Daniel

1995 LPGA Stat Leaders

Match the LPGA Tour player with the honor she won or the statistical category she led in 1995.

1. Player of the Year
2. Rookie of the Year
3. Putting Leader
4. Eagle Leader
5. Greens in Regulation
6. Sand Saves
7. Birdie Leader
8. Driving Accuracy
9. Top 10 Finishes
10. Tour Scoring Leader

a. Kay Cockerill
b. Betsy King
c. Meg Mallon
d. Annika Sorenstam
e. Kelly Robbins
f. Nancy Ramsbottom
g. Caroline Pierce
h. Pat Hurst

1995 LPGA Stat Leaders

Answers
1. d. Annika Sorenstam
2. h. Pat Hurst
3. a. Kay Cockerill
4. e. Kelly Robbins
5. c. Meg Mallon
6. g. Caroline Pierce
7. b. Betsy King
8. f. Nancy Ramsbottom
9. b. Betsy King (13/26)
10. d. Annika Sorenstam

LPGA Tour Driving Distance

Match the LPGA player with her average driving distance in 1995.

1. 265.2   a. Michelle McGann

2. 261.6   b. Kelly Robbins

3. 256.1   c. Karen Lunn

4. 252.5   d. Jane Geddes

5. 252.4   e. Laura Davies

LPGA Tour Driving Distance

Answers
1. e. Laura Davies
2. b. Kelly Robbins
3. a. Michelle McGann
4. c. Karen Lunn
5. d. Jane Geddes

1995 PGA

1995 PGA Tour Winners Match

Match the PGA player with the tournament(s) he won in 1995.

1. Western Open
2. PGA Championship
3. World Series of Golf
4. British Open
5. US Open
6. The Masters
7. The International
8. Byron Nelson Classic
9. Bob Hope Classic
10. The Players Championship

a. Steve Elkington
b. Lee Janzen
c. John Daly
d. Billy Mayfair
e. Kenny Perry
f. Ben Crenshaw
g. Greg Norman
h. Ernie Els
i. Corey Pavin

1995 PGA Tour Winners Match

Answers
1. d. Billy Mayfair
2. a. Steve Elkington
3. g. Greg Norman
4. c. John Daly
5. i. Corey Pavin
6. f. Ben Crenshaw
7. b. Lee Janzen
8. h. Ernie Els
9. e. Kenny Perry
10. b. Lee Janzen

1995 PGA Tournament $$$$

Match the 1995 Tour event with the winner's purse.

1. PGA Championship   a. $200,000

2. British   b. $396,000

3. US Open   c. $540,000

4. The Masters   d. $360,000

5. The Players Championship   e. $350,000

1995 PGA Tournament $$$

Answers
1. d.
2. a.
3. e.
4. b.
5. c.

1995 PGA Tour Money Leaders

Match the Tour player with the amount of money he won in 1995.

1. $1,654,959
2. $1,543,192
3. $1,378,966
4. $1,340,079
5. $1,254,352
6. $1,111,999
7. $1,075,057
8. $1,057,241
9. $1,018,713
10. $914,129

a. Billy Mayfair
b. Jim Gallagher, Jr
c. Steve Elkington
d. Greg Norman
e. Davis Love III
f. Vijay Singh
g. Lee Janzen
h. Peter Jacobsen
i. Mark O'Meara
j. Corey Pavin

1995 PGA Tour Money Leaders

Answers
1. d. Greg Norman
2. a. Billy Mayfair
3. g. Lee Janzen
4. j. Corey Pavin
5. c. Steve Elkington
6. e. Davis Love III
7. h. Peter Jacobsen
8. b. Jim Gallagher, Jr.
9. f. Vijay Singh
10. i. Mark O'Meara

Career Earnings Match

Match the PGA player with the rank and $$$ amount of his career PGA earnings through the 1995 Tour Championship.

1. $9,592,829   a. Corey Pavin

2. $9,337,998   b. Curtis Strange

3. $7,389,479   c. Ben Crenshaw

4. $7,338,119   d. Tom Kite

5. $7,188,408   e. Tom Watson

6. $7,175,523   f. Greg Norman

7. $7,072,113   g. Paul Azinger

8. $6,957,324   h. Nick Price

9. $6,845,235   i. Payne Stewart

10. $6,791,618   j. Fred Couples

Career Earnings Match

Answers
1. f
2. d
3. i
4. h
5. j
6. a
7. e
8. g
9. c
10. b

More 1995 Tour Winners

Match these PGA players with the tournament they won in 1995.

1. Pebble Beach Pro-Am
2. Canadian Open
3. BellSouth Classic
4. Doral Open
5. Greater Greensboro Open
6. MCI Classic
7. Freeport-McMoran Classic
8. Nestle Invitational
9. Phoenix Open
10. Northern Telecom Open

a. J. Gallagher Jr.
b. M. Calcavecchia
c. Loren Roberts
d. Mark O'Meara
e. Vijay Singh
f. Bob Tway
g. Phil Mickelson
h. Peter Jacobsen
i. Davis Love III
j. Nick Faldo

More 1995 Tour Winners

Answers
1. h. Peter Jacobsen
2. d. Mark O'Meara
3. b. M. Calcavecchia
4. j. Nick Faldo
5. a. J. Gallagher Jr.
6. f. Bob Tway
7. i. Davis Love III
8. c. Loren Roberts
9. e. Vijay Singh
10. g. Phil Mickelson

PGA Tour Scoring Leaders

Match each Tour player with his 1995 average 18-hole score.

1. 69.06
2. 69.59
3. 69.81(tie)
4. 69.81(tie)
5. 69.85(tie)
6. 69.85(tie)
7. 69.92
8. 69.93
9. 69.99
10. 70.03

a. Steve Elkington
b. Scott Simpson
c. Vijay Singh
d. Greg Norman
e. Nick Faldo
f. Ernie Els
g. Bob Tway
h. Nick Price
i. Peter Jacobsen
j. Tom Lehman

PGA Tour Scoring Leaders

Answers
1. d. Greg Norman
2. a. Steve Elkington
3. f. Ernie Els
4. h. Nick Price
5. e. Nick Faldo
6. j. Tom Lehman
7. c. Vijay Singh
8. g. Bob Tway
9. b. Scott Simpson
10. i. Peter Jacobsen

1995 Tour Stat Leaders

Match each player with the statistical category he led on the 1995 Tour.

1. Putting Leader   a. Kelly Gibson

2. Eagle Leader   b. Steve Lowery

3. Greens in Regulation   c. Jim Furyk

4. Sand Saves   d. Billy Mayfair

5. Birdie Leader   e. Lennie Clements

1995 Tour Stat Leaders

Answers
1. c. Jim Furyk (1.708)
2. a. Kelly Gibson (16)
3. e. Lennie Clements (72.3)
4. d. Billy Mayfair (68.6%)
5. b. Steve Lowery (410)

PGA Driving Distance Leaders

Match each player with his 1995 average driving distance.

1. 289.0   a. Dennis Paulson

2. 284.6   b. Vijay Singh

3. 284.1   c. Davis Love III

4. 283.5   d. John Daly

5. 280.2   e. Kelly Gibson

PGA Driving Distance Leaders

Answers

1. d. John Daly
2. c. Davis Love III
3. a. Dennis Paulson
4. b. Vijay Singh
5. e. Kelly Gibson

PGA Tour Driving Accuracy

Match each player with his 1995 percentage of drives in the fairway.

1. 81.3%   a. Fred Funk

2. 80.3%   b. Bruce Lietzke

3. 79.6%   c. David Edwards

4. 79.1%   d. Larry Mize

5. 78.8%   e. Doug Tewell

PGA Tour Driving Accuracy

Answers
 1. a. Fred Funk
 2. e. Doug Tewell
 3. d. Larry Mize
 4. c. David Edwards
 5. b. Bruce Lietzke

$$$ in the '90s Match

Match the PGA Tour player with his earnings during the '90s as of January 1, 1996.

1. $6,507,035   a. Paul Azinger

2. $5,961,123   b. Fred Couples

3. $5,350,665   c. Corey Pavin

4. $4,615,428   d. Nick Price

5. $4,214,670   e. Greg Norman

$$$ in the '90's Match

Answers
1. e
2. d
3. c
4. b
5. a